INSIDE
LIGHTNING

by Melissa Stewart

Illustrations by Cynthia Shaw

STERLING CHILDREN'S BOOKS
New York

STERLING CHILDREN'S BOOKS
New York

An Imprint of Sterling Publishing
387 Park Avenue South
New York, NY 10016

Designed by Anke Stohlmann Design.

ISBN 978-1-4027-5878-2 (hardcover)
ISBN 978-1-4027-8949-6 (flexibound)

Distributed in Canada by Sterling Publishing
c/o Canadian Manda Group, 165 Dufferin Street
Toronto, Ontario, Canada M6K 3H6
Distributed in the United Kingdom by GMC Distribution Services
Castle Place, 166 High Street, Lewes, East Sussex, England BN7 1XU
Distributed in Australia by Capricorn Link (Australia) Pty. Ltd.
P.O. Box 704, Windsor, NSW 2756, Australia

For information about custom editions, special sales, and premium and corporate purchases, please contact Sterling Special Sales at 800-805-5489 or specialsales@sterlingpublishing.com.

Printed in China
Lot#:
10 9 8 7 6 5 4 3 2 1
07/11

www.sterlingpublishing.com/kids

FIRE FROM THE SKY

Bright. Beautiful. Dramatic. Dangerous. Lightning is all of these things—and more. It's one of the most amazing features of the natural world.

Lightning kills about two thousand people on Earth every year. But some scientists think none of us would be here without it. They say lightning provided the sparks of energy that made life on our planet possible. As lightning bolts raced through Earth's early atmosphere, they set off chemical reactions. Those reactions created materials that our planet's first creatures needed to survive.

Lightning bolts can ignite wildfires that devastate acre after acre of forests and grasslands. But those flashes from the sky also provided early humans with their most important survival tool—fire! More than 1.4 million years ago, our ancient ancestors began using fire to cook animal meat and to light their way at night. During the day, early humans worked hard to keep their fires going. They never knew when or where lightning would strike, providing them a new source of flames. According to some scientists, people probably didn't figure out how to make fire themselves until about 9,000 years ago.

Without lightning, our ancestors would have had a much tougher time surviving. And if the fiery bolts hadn't supported Earth's earliest creatures, we might not even exist. Lightning is much more than a dazzling display of flickering light. Turn the page to learn more about it.

WHAT IS LIGHTNING?

Ancient Ideas About Lightning

In most of the world's early civilizations, people told stories to explain earthquakes, eclipses, meteor showers, tsunamis, and other natural events. In many cases, the people in these ancient cultures thought lightning was made by the gods they worshipped.

Ancient Aztecs

The Aztecs lived in what is now Mexico. They believed that Tlaloc, their god of rain and water, used lightning to make people sick.

Ancient China

Lei Kung was a Chinese god who chased away evil spirits and punished criminals. He made thunder with his hammer, and his wife, Tian Mu, made lightning with her mirrors.

Ancient Egypt

Set was the Egyptian god of the sky, deserts, winds, storms, and destruction. He made lightning with his iron spear.

Ancient Greece

The Greeks believed that three one-eyed monsters called Cyclops made lightning for Zeus, the king of the gods. When Zeus was angry, he hurled lightning bolts down to Earth.

Ancient Mesopotamia

The Mesopotamians lived in an area that is now Iraq, and parts of Iran, Syria, and Turkey. Their god Adad, master of weather and storms, carried a staff (a long stick) shaped like a lightning bolt. He flung lightning through the air while riding his bull across the sky.

Ancient Scandinavia

A thousand years ago, the Vikings believed that during thunderstorms their god Thor rode through the heavens in a chariot pulled by two goats. Lightning flashed whenever he threw his red-hot hammer at enemies.

CONTENTS

How to read this book

This book is different from most books you read. Many of its pages fold out—or flip up! To know where to read next, follow arrows like these ⬆, and look for page numbers to help you find your place. Happy exploring!

What a Shock!

In the early 1700s, many people in Europe thought lightning was caused by poisonous gases that exploded in the air. They had no idea that the deadly zigzagging bolts are just more powerful versions of the gentle electric jolts we all feel when we shuffle across a carpet and then touch a metal object. Before people could understand lightning, they needed to learn more about electricity. And thanks to a newly invented device called the friction machine, that was beginning to happen.

People who called themselves electricians used friction machines to perform all kinds of tricks. As an electrician spun the machine's crank, an electric charge built up on a glass tube. When the electrician placed a metal rod close to the glass tube, sparks danced through the air. And when a volunteer held a finger close to the glass tube, ZAP!

Around 1734, Georg Matthias Bose, a German scientist, hosted a shocking dinner party. As his guests ate, he touched a charged glass rod to the table and sparks flew between the table and the guests' forks.

A few years later, a French scientist named Abbé Jean-Antoine Nollet heard about another new invention—the Leyden jar, which can hold a larger charge than a glass rod. To amuse King Louis XV, Nollet asked 180 soldiers to stand in a line and hold hands. When the man at the end of the line touched a Leyden jar, BAM! The entire army jerked to attention.

The Leyden jar was invented by Pieter van Musschenbroek of Leyden, Netherlands.

Newsflash!

The word *electric* comes from the Latin term *electrum*, which means "amber." Amber is fossilized tree resin. Around 1600, British scientist William Gilbert discovered that he could produce electric charges by rubbing amber with wool or fur.

Lightning strikes, like these in Redrock, Arizona, can be especially dramatic at dusk.

Newsflash!

Lightning strikes our planet about one hundred times every second. Each bolt zaps the ground with enough energy to light up a 100-watt lightbulb for three months!

The Key and the Kite

By the 1740s, electricians had begun performing in Colonial America. Benjamin Franklin saw one of them and became fascinated by electricity. He wanted to try some of the tricks.

In one experiment, Franklin made an "electric spider" by attaching eight cotton threads to a piece of cork. When the spider was suspended from a silk thread, it mysteriously jumped back and forth between a charged Leyden jar and a wire.

Next, Franklin asked a lady and a gentleman to stand on some wax. (Like silk, wax doesn't conduct electricity.) When one person held a Leyden jar and the other held a wire, both people felt a small shock. When the man and woman tried to kiss, sparks shot between their lips. Yowzah!

As Franklin experimented with electricity, a revolutionary idea struck him. Maybe the giant sparks of lightning that come from thunderclouds are the same as the smaller sparks he was creating in his workshop. Maybe lightning was electricity.

To find out, Franklin built a kite with a wire on top to attract lightning. He tied a key to the end of the kite string and then attached a silk ribbon. He hoped that if lightning were electricity and a bolt struck the wire attached to the kite, the electric charge would travel down the kite string to the metal key. Because silk doesn't conduct electricity, Ben thought that as long as the ribbon stayed dry, he would be safe.

As a thunderstorm raged in June 1752, Ben and his son, William, stood inside a shed and flew the kite out the doorway. When a low cloud passed overhead, loose threads on the kite string popped straight up. Was the experiment working? To find out, Ben moved his hand toward the key.

Zap! Out flew a bright spark. Ben had his proof. Lightning really was electricity. It was a giant electric spark.

This is an artist's representation of Benjamin Franklin conducting his famous kite experiment. The experiment proved that lightning is electricity.

WHERE AND WHEN DOES LIGHTNING STRIKE?

Thunderstorms that produce lightning are most common in tropical areas. The brilliant bolts flashed over the mouth of the Mdumbi River in Transkei, South Africa in 2005.

Thunderstorms—and the lightning they produce—can strike anyplace on Earth. In fact, lightning flashes somewhere around the world about six thousand times every minute. That adds up to more than eight million strikes every day.

Thunderstorms are most common in places with warm, steamy weather. That means tropical areas near the equator have a lot more thunderstorms than places closer to the North and South poles.

Storm's a Brewin'

It's midsummer, and each day is hotter and more humid than the last. These are just the right conditions for the formation of thunderheads—the kind of clouds that produce thunderstorms with bright bolts of lightning.

4 As clouds form, hot air near the ground rises faster and faster. And it travels higher and higher. With air shooting upward at 60 miles (96 km) per hour, a thunderhead can stretch more than 11 miles (17 km) high in just a few minutes. When that towering cloud darkens to gray and then black, a thunderstorm is about to strike.

1 All day long, the sun's bright rays beat down. They heat up the ground and the air just above it.

3 When the hot air comes into contact with cold, dry air high in the atmosphere, it loses some of its heat. Since cool air can't hold as much moisture as hot air, water vapor begins to condense from the air. It changes from a gas into the tiny water droplets that form puffy, white clouds.

This electrician (far right) has used silk cords (which don't conduct electricity) to hoist a boy into the air. When the boy places his feet on the friction machine and touches a glass rod, sparks shoot out in every direction.

2 By noon, the hot air starts to rise up into the sky.

Newsflash!

Most thunderheads rain down on an area smaller than the average American town and last for less than thirty minutes. But sometimes many, many thunderclouds form in a long line, causing larger storms that last longer.

Heavy rain falls from two distinct parts of this thunderstorm in Tucson, Arizona.

All Charged Up

Inside a thunderhead, water droplets budge and bump, crash and clump. They grow larger and larger, heavier and heavier, until they plummet to the ground. The rain may begin as a gentle sprinkle, but it soon picks up speed.

At about the same time, some of the water vapor inside the cloud starts to freeze into ice. As ice and rain fall down through the thunderhead, they cool the cloud. Hot air is still rising from the ground, but it no longer shoots straight up to the top of the cloud, as it did when the thunderhead was forming. Instead, the hot air and cold air swirl together, tossing around the ice inside the thunderhead.

So what happens next? Scientists don't know for sure, but they do have some ideas. According to the most popular theory, as the pieces of ice inside a thunderhead are hurled back and forth, up and down, they smash into one another. During these collisions, the ice becomes electrically charged. Scientists think the larger chunks of ice become negatively charged, while the smaller slivers become positively charged.

The larger, heavier pieces of ice fall toward the bottom of the cloud, but air currents lift the smaller, lighter pieces up. Over time, the top of the thunderhead becomes positively charged and the bottom becomes negatively charged. Then it's just a matter of time before lightning starts flashing through the sky.

A spectacular thunderhead forms over Winnipeg, Manitoba, Canada.

A CLOSER LOOK AT LIGHTNING

From Cloud to Ground

As negative electric charges build at the bottom of a thunderhead, some of them leak out of the cloud. Soon the air around the bottom of the cloud is negatively charged too. All those negative charges begin to affect objects on the ground.

Most of the time, the ground has a neutral charge—the positive and negative charges are about equal, so they balance each other out. But that changes as a thunderhead forms. Negative electric charges attract positive electric charges. And they repel, or push away, other negative charges. So over time, the ground—and tall objects like trees, flagpoles, and church steeples—beneath the thunderhead becomes positively charged.

When the difference between the negative charge at the bottom of the cloud and the positive charge on the ground is great enough, a stream of electricity bursts out of the cloud and plunges downward.

Newsflash!

Most cloud-to-ground lightning strikes transport negative energy to the ground, but occasionally, strikes deliver positive charges. Positive lightning bolts come from the top of thunderheads. Some scientists think that positive lightning strikes are common in thunderclouds that spin out tornadoes.

Even though these lightning bolts at Ayers Rock in Australia's Uluru National Park are only about as wide as your finger, they may be up to 10 miles (16 km) long.

Lightning Step-by-Step

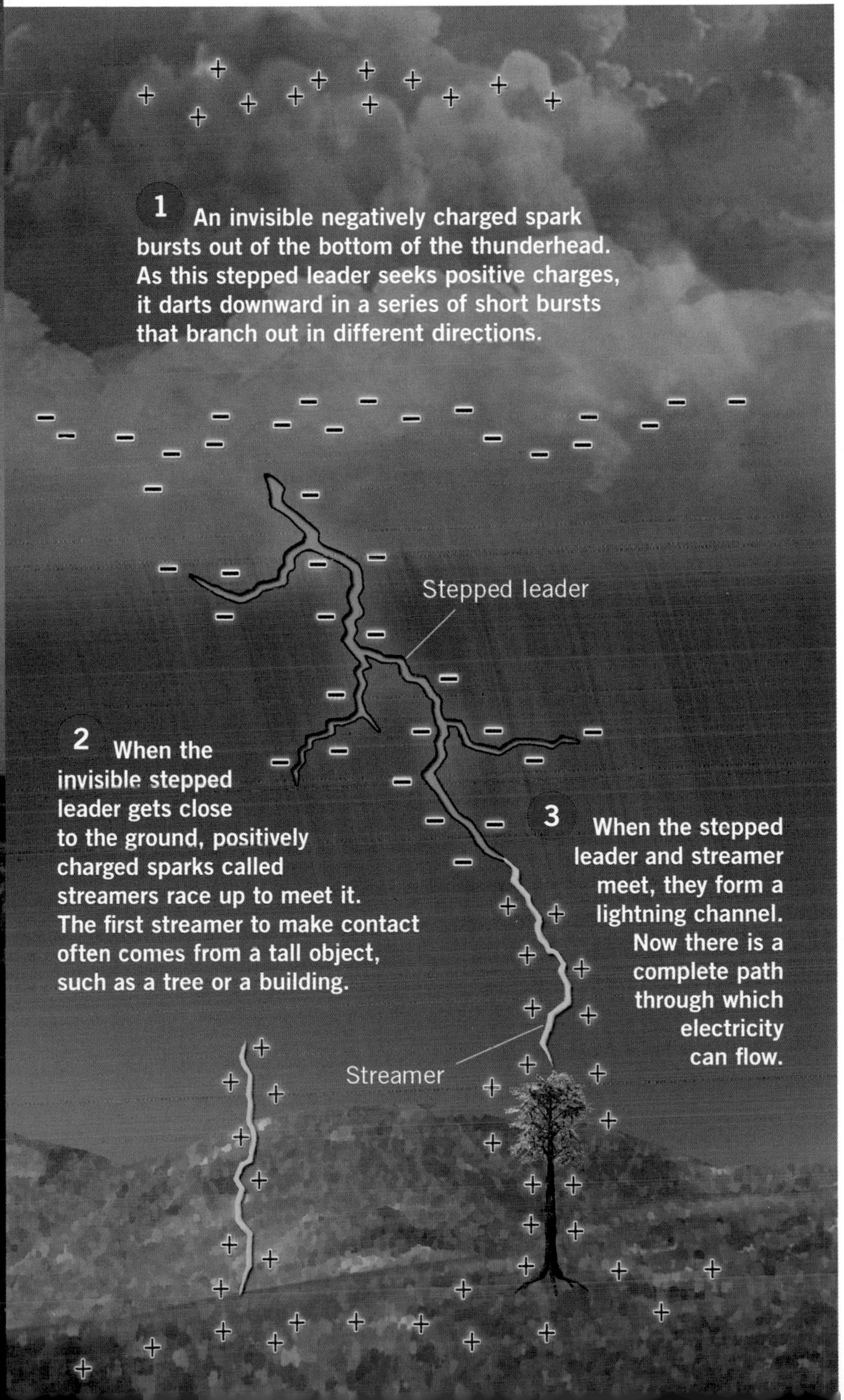

1 An invisible negatively charged spark bursts out of the bottom of the thunderhead. As this stepped leader seeks positive charges, it darts downward in a series of short bursts that branch out in different directions.

Stepped leader

2 When the invisible stepped leader gets close to the ground, positively charged sparks called streamers race up to meet it. The first streamer to make contact often comes from a tall object, such as a tree or a building.

3 When the stepped leader and streamer meet, they form a lightning channel. Now there is a complete path through which electricity can flow.

Streamer

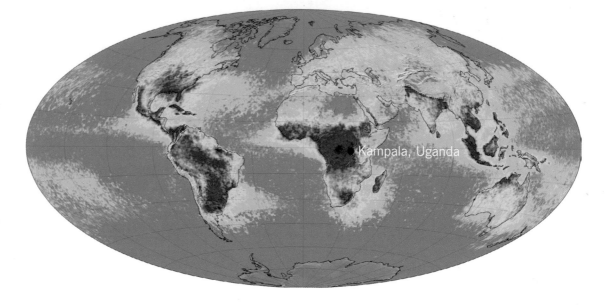

This map shows the frequency of lightning strikes all over the world. Regions shaded red receive the most strikes. Orange and yellow areas are next highest in strikes. Green, blue, and purple regions experience even fewer strikes. Gray areas receive the least number.

Kampala, Uganda

Newsflash!

When lightning flashes, it heats gases in the air. Two of those gases, nitrogen and oxygen, combine to form a natural fertilizer called nitrous oxide. When nitrous oxide mixes with raindrops, it falls to the ground, and makes the soil richer. That means lightning helps plants all over the world grow big and strong.

Kampala, Uganda, in East Africa has more thunderstorms—and more lightning strikes—than any other place on Earth. On average, thunderstorms light up the sky 240 days each year. That's like having a thunderstorm pour down on you every single day for more than eight months!

In many parts of North America, thunderstorms are common on hot, humid summer afternoons and evenings. But Florida is the lightning capital of the United States. Scientists call the area from Orlando and Tampa south to Fort Myers and Lake Okeechobee the "lightning belt." A single thunderstorm in this region can produce hundreds of lightning strikes.

Lightning strikes can help to enrich soil.

How Charges Form

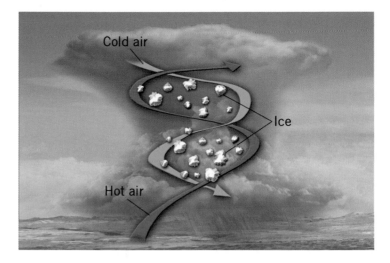

Cold air

Ice

Hot air

1 When hot air and cold air swirl around inside a cloud, ice particles go along for the ride.

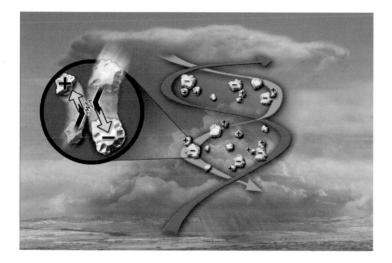

2 Eventually, ice particles begin to collide. Scientists believe that larger pieces become negatively charged (-) and smaller pieces become positively charged (+).

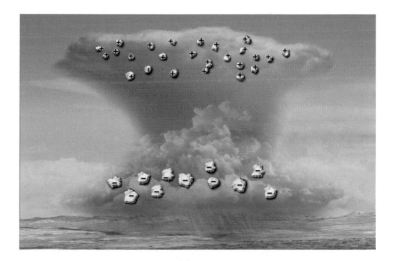

3 Larger, negatively charged pieces of ice congregate near the bottom of the cloud. Smaller, positively charged pieces of ice congregate at the top of the cloud.

On April 18, 2010, people saw lightning bolts zigzagging down from ash clouds erupting from the Eyjafjallajokull volcano in Iceland.

Surprising Sparks

· · · · · · · · · · · · · · · · ·

Most of the lightning flashes we see occur during thunderstorms, but snowstorms, dust storms, wildfires, and volcanic eruptions can also trigger lightning.

It turns out that shards of ice aren't the only tiny particles that can build up electrical charges. Sand grains, soot, and volcanic ash can too.

As these particles collide, some become positively charged, and others become negatively charged. For reasons scientists don't fully understand, the different charges move in opposite directions. The charges build up until sizzling strokes of lightning streak through the sky in a dazzling display.

Newsflash!

Everyone knows that lightning can be dangerous, but some people are terrified that they will be struck. Scientists use the term *keraunophobia* (kee-rah-noh-FOH-bee-ah) to describe an irrational fear of lightning. *Brontophobia* (brahn-toh-FOH-bee-ah) is an overwhelming fear of thunder.

Lightning travels up to 60,000 miles (96,500 km) per hour. At that speed, each bright bolt lasts only an instant. If you could view lightning in slow motion, you'd see that each flickering flash involves a series of steps.

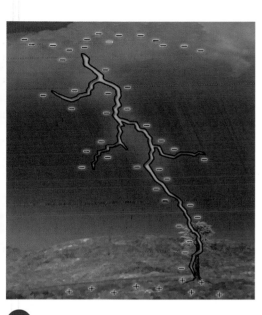

4 Negative charges from the thunder-head rush into the ground and discharge, or release their energy.

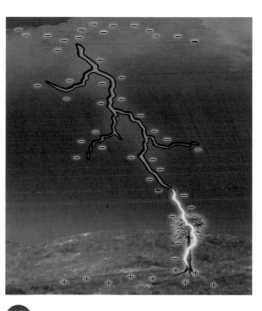

5 Because the negative charges at the bottom of the lightning channel discharge first, the light moves from the ground up.

6 This surge of electricity, called a *return stroke*, travels so quickly that the air around it glows—and we see it as the flash we call *lightning*.

7 The negative charges move far too fast for our eyes to see, so to us, the whole path seems to light up at once.

8 After a tiny pause, a new leader, called a *dart leader*, enters the lightning channel and travels directly toward the ground.

9 As it discharges, we see a second flicker of light. Most lightning strikes consist of three or four separate return strokes, but sometimes there are more than twenty.

This photograph captures a severe thunderstorm over Linz, Austria.

Crash, Crackle, Rumble, and Roll

During a return stroke, the lightning channel blasts the air with 50,000 degrees Fahrenheit (28,000 degrees Celsius) of heat energy. That's five times hotter than the surface of the sun.

As the air around the channel heats up, it expands rapidly, producing a violent shockwave that explodes outward in every direction. The shockwave creates a series of intense sound waves that we hear as thunder. If the storm is close by, we hear a loud crackling boom. If it is farther away, we hear a low rolling rumble.

Even though lightning creates thunder, we usually don't see the flash of light and hear the thunderous crash at exactly the same moment. That's because light travels much faster than sound. Light surges through the sky at 186,000 miles (297,600 km) per second, but sound travels just 1,000 feet (305 meters) per second.

You can figure out how far away a thunderstorm is by counting the seconds between the time your eyes see a flash of lightning and your ears hear the thunder. For every five seconds you count, the storm is about 1 mile (1.6 km) away.

This photograph captures a severe thunderstorm over Linz, Austria.

Crash, Crackle, Rumble, and Roll

During a return stroke, the lightning channel blasts the air with 50,000 degrees Fahrenheit (28,000 degrees Celsius) of heat energy. That's five times hotter than the surface of the sun.

As the air around the channel heats up, it expands rapidly, producing a violent shockwave that explodes outward in every direction. The shockwave creates a series of intense sound waves that we hear as thunder. If the storm is close by, we hear a loud crackling boom. If it is farther away, we hear a low rolling rumble.

Even though lightning creates thunder, we usually don't see the flash of light and hear the thunderous crash at exactly the same moment. That's because light travels much faster than sound. Light surges through the sky at 186,000 miles (297,600 km) per second, but sound travels just 1,000 feet (305 meters) per second.

You can figure out how far away a thunderstorm is by counting the seconds between the time your eyes see a flash of lightning and your ears hear the thunder. For every five seconds you count, the storm is about 1 mile (1.6 km) away.

Lightning travels up to 60,000 miles (96,500 km) per hour. At that speed, each bright bolt lasts only an instant. If you could view lightning in slow motion, you'd see that each flickering flash involves a series of steps.

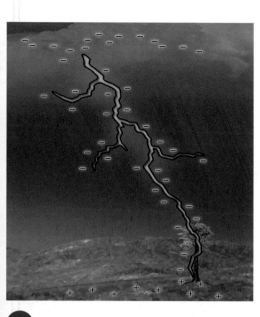

4 Negative charges from the thunderhead rush into the ground and discharge, or release their energy.

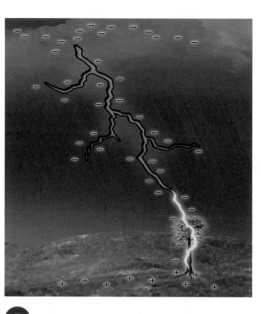

5 Because the negative charges at the bottom of the lightning channel discharge first, the light moves from the ground up.

6 This surge of electricity, called a *return stroke*, travels so quickly that the air around it glows—and we see it as the flash we call *lightning*.

7 The negative charges move far too fast for our eyes to see, so to us, the whole path seems to light up at once.

8 After a tiny pause, a new leader, called a *dart leader*, enters the lightning channel and travels directly toward the ground.

9 As it discharges, we see a second flicker of light. Most lightning strikes consist of three or four separate return strokes, but sometimes there are more than twenty.

All Kinds of Lightning

When you think of lightning, you probably picture a streak of light racing through the sky, but not all lightning strokes look the same. Believe it or not, lightning comes in streaks, forks, sheets, balls, and more. Lift the flap to learn more about some of the strangest lightning on Earth.

Some thunderstorms produce bolts of streak lightning. They race to the ground as single bright wiggly lines.

Two dramatic bolts of forked lightning illuminate a Sonoran Desert ridge covered with saguaro cactuses.

We Were There!

In 1972, lightning struck Bruce and Dorothy Stewart's home in Southampton, Massachusetts. "I saw a bluish-white ball of light float in through the open living room window," said Dorothy. "It was the size of a basketball, and it blew a light bulb in a nearby lamp. My skin tingled as it slowly drifted to the middle of the room. Then it dropped toward the floor and disappeared."

Bruce was in the basement. "I saw it come down through the ceiling almost right in front of my face. It didn't make a hole or burn anything, but it did blow an overhead light. Then it slowly bobbed and floated across the basement and faded away."

Freaky Flashes

Sheet

This sheet lightning over Mt. Wellington in Australia seems to instantly brighten a wide area of sky. The lightning is so far away that you can't see the bolt. What you see is the light reflected off clouds or scattered by water droplets in the air.

St. Elmo's Fire

An eerie blue, green, or purplish glow may flicker around tall objects, such as the tip of this antenna at the Langmuir Laboratory for Atmospheric Research in Socorro, New Mexico, as negative electric charges in the air are pulled toward the positively charged object. This effect, called St. Elmo's fire, is named after Erasmus, a Christian saint who was believed to protect sailors.

Ball

In this historical etching, four well-dressed gentlemen are startled by ball lightning—a glowing sphere of light that can be as small as an apple or as large as a soccer ball. This ball of electricity hovers in place or floats through the air for up to several minutes. Then it fades away or explodes with a loud pop.

Bolt from the Blue

A bolt from the blue is a lightning strike that seems to come from a clear blue sky. In this photo, the bolt arcs from the top of a cloud to the horizon off the coast of the Bahamas. The lightning strike is positively charged energy released from the top of a distant thunderhead. It may travel horizontally for several miles before swerving downward to connect with a streamer.

From Cloud to Cloud

Cloud-to-ground lightning can hurt people and destroy property, so scientists spend a lot of time studying it. But believe it or not, only about one-quarter of all lightning bolts strike the earth. Most of the electrical charges that build up inside thunderheads never leave the sky.

At the beginning of a storm, the negative charges at the bottom of a thunderhead are usually attracted to positive charges at the top of the same cloud. This kind of lightning makes a thunderhead seem to glow from within.

As a storm continues, some of a thunderhead's negative charges may form lightning channels with streamers that have jumped from the tops of nearby clouds. This kind of lightning never touches the ground, but it can be very dangerous for airplanes in flight.

Cloud-to-cloud lightning flashes over the African savanna.

Lt. Colonel Rankin fell through a thunderhead similar to this one. After rain starts to fall from the thunderhead, the cloud begins to spread out and lose height.

I Was There!

In 1959, the engine on Lieutenant Colonel William H. Rankin's F8U Crusader supersonic jet stalled, and he was forced to eject 37,000 feet (11,280 m) above Norfolk, Virginia. During his descent, Rankin fell through a thunderhead.

"I was pushed up, pushed down, stretched, slammed, and pounded," recalls Rankin. "I was in an angry ocean of boiling clouds, blacks, grays, and whites spilling over each other, into each other, digesting each other . . . I saw [lightning] in every shape imaginable. . . . it appeared mainly as a huge bluish sheet, several feet thick, sometimes sticking close to me in pairs, like the blades of a scissors, and I had the distinct feeling that I was being sliced in two."

When Rankin landed he was cold, wet, and exhausted, but he had only a few minor injuries.

Sprites, Elves, and Jets

During some thunderstorms, the most brilliant light displays occur high above the clouds. Scientists are still trying to learn what causes these mysterious lights. They are difficult to study because they are so short-lived, but if you happen to be in the right place at the right time, you can even see them from the ground.

Elve
Intense lightning strikes can also trigger flat disks of dim reddish light to form about 60 miles (96 km) above the earth. The light of an elve radiates outward in every direction, spreading over an area of sky up to 250 miles (400 km) wide.

Red sprite
Immediately after a very energetic bolt of lightning strikes the ground, ghostly red light may shoot straight up from the top of a thunderhead. Some red sprites soar up to 60 miles (96 km) into the atmosphere.

Blue jet

Blue jets are dim, blue streaks of light. They look like quick puffs of smoke that burst out of a thunderhead, arc upward, and then fade away. Blue jets can climb as high as 30 miles (48 km) into the atmosphere.

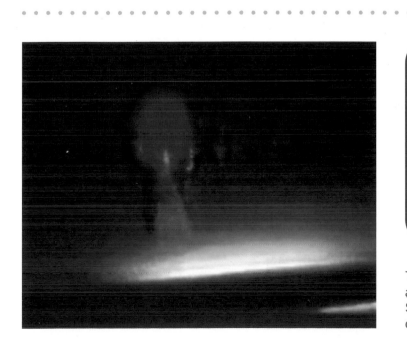

Newsflash!

For more than a century, people had been reporting colorful flickers of light shooting straight up from thunderheads, but scientists were skeptical. Then in 1989, researchers finally caught these eerie illuminations on videotape. Around the same time, astronauts photographed a red sprite from the space shuttle.

This stunning color photo of a sprite was taken from an airplane in 1994. Researchers from National Aeronautics and Space Administration (NASA) and the University of Alaska captured the image with an intensified color TV camera.

trouble, but about one hundred are deadly. Lightning kills more people than tornadoes or hurricanes.

Here's the good news: Almost 90 percent of all lightning victims survive. Many escape with just minor burns. Some suffer long-term health problems, including memory loss, dizziness, muscles spasms, and numbness.

Most lightning victims are struck while doing such outdoor activities as hunting, fishing, hiking, golfing, swimming, or boating. On average, the greatest number of Americans are struck each year in Florida, and the fewest are struck in Oregon.

Newsflash!

Most lightning survivors wake up dazed and confused, and some are shocked to find themselves completely naked. Sometimes the jolt of negatively charged energy can blow a person's clothes right off his or her body. What a shock!

Staying Safe

According to lightning researchers, if you can hear thunder, then you're at risk of being struck by lightning. They suggest following the 30/30 Rule: If there is less than *30* seconds between a lightning strike and the thunder that accompanies it, seek cover immediately. Be sure to stay indoors or in a safe, sheltered area, for at least *30* minutes after the storm's last peal of thunder.

If you're stuck outside during a thunderstorm, keep heading for safety unless you feel your skin tingle or your hair stand on end. That means the air around you is positively charged, and lightning may be about to strike. Crouch down low and balance on the balls of your feet. Locking your hands behind your neck will help you stay balanced. Because lightning seeks a path to the ground, you'll be safest if very little of your body is touching the earth.

Newsflash!

According to the *Guinness Book of World Records*, Roy "Dooms" Sullivan was the most lightning-prone person to ever walk the earth. Between 1942 and 1977, the park ranger was struck by lightning seven times.

We Were There!

On August 20, 1975, Sean, Michael, Jeff, and Mary McQuilken set out to climb Moro Rock in California's Sequoia National Park. The sky was overcast with patches of dark clouds, and it was raining lightly. Just after reaching the top, the McQuilkens noticed that their hair was standing on end, and Mary snapped this photo of her brothers Sean (left) and Michael (right).

Moments later, the temperature dropped and hail began to fall. As the McQuilkens hurried down Moro Rock, lightning struck. Michael remembers being "immersed in the brightest light I have ever seen. I remember feeling weightless. A deafening explosion followed, and I found myself on the ground." Although Sean was knocked unconscious, all four children survived the strike. Another hiker wasn't so lucky.

Unlucky Strikes

Lightning does more than harm people. It also causes more than $5 billion in property damage to private homes every year. It knocks over trees and telephone poles, starts wildfires, and destroys buildings. The fiery flashes are also responsible for one-third of all power outages in North America.

Trees

Lightning is attracted to tall objects, but that's not the only reason trees are at risk. Trees contain large amounts of watery tree sap. Sap is a good conductor of electricity. A live tree conducts electric charges hundreds of times better than a dead, dried out tree.

When lightning hits a tree, it may merely rip a line down the trunk, or it may blow the tree to bits. The damage depends on the strength of the stroke and the kind of tree.

Newsflash!

Oak trees are struck more often than other kinds of trees because they contain more water.

Wildfires

Half of all wildfires in the western United States are caused by summertime thunderstorms. During hot weather, grass and other small plants on the ground dry out. When lightning strikes a tree or the ground, sparks fly in every direction, and some of them ignite the plants. Thunderstorm winds spread the flames quickly, and soon the fire is out of control.

Even though wildfires destroy millions of acres of forests and grasslands every year, many natural areas depend on these blazes. By burning brush on the ground, wildfires create space for new plants to grow. In addition, some kinds of seeds can't sprout without fire. For example, some pine cones won't open and release their seeds unless they are heated by fire.

Many people are struck by lightning while fishing because metal fishing poles can attract electricity.

I Was There!

In May 1991, fifteen-year-old Tal Alter attended a lacrosse match at St. Albans School in Washington, DC. When referees called a rain delay, Tal and several other people took cover under a tree. A few minutes later, lightning struck the tree. "[T]here was a loud explosion and a big orange flash," recalls Tal.

Tal was one of a dozen people affected by a "splash" of lighting that shot up from the tree's roots. "I just remember being sent back to the ground and just lying there and not being able to feel my legs and not knowing exactly what had happened." Luckily, Tal recovered completely from the lightning strike.

Buildings

Lightning strikes millions of homes and office buildings all over the world every year. Most of the time, the jolt of energy does very little damage. It might fry a television or zap a computer. But some lightning strikes can be much more severe. They can blast roofs open and blow out entire walls. They can even start electrical fires that burn buildings to the ground.

Most modern homes have lightning rods to protect them from bolts of electricity. These devices, which were invented by Benjamin Franklin, limit lightning damage by attracting negative charges and safely conducting them to the ground.

LIGHTNING SCIENTISTS AT WORK

· ·

Lightning Does Strike Twice

· ·

Bolts of lightning are drawn to the lightning rod atop New York City's Empire State Building.

Have you ever heard the expression, "lightning doesn't strike twice"? Don't believe it!

Here's the truth: Tall objects, such as buildings and trees, are often struck again and again. The Empire State Building in New York City attracts about 100 lightning strikes every year. That's because architects designed the 102-story skyscraper to protect the surrounding area. It has a 203-foot (62-m) tall pinnacle with a lightning rod on top.

During the 1930s and 1940s, scientists set up experiments on the Empire State Building to study lightning strikes and the electricity associated with them.

Newsflash!

The Empire State Building is made of 60,000 tons of steel and 10 million bricks. It was the world's tallest building when it was completed in 1931. Today it is the fifteenth tallest.

Don't try this at home! Some people enjoy observing lightning using powerful spotting scopes and long-distance camera equipment. But this can be dangerous if the storm suddenly changes direction.

CAUTION
LIGHTNING STRIKE AREA

PLEASE SEEK COVER OFF THIS JETTY
PRIOR TO THE APPROACH OF STORMS.
INJURIES HAVE OCCURED ON THIS
STRUCTURE DUE TO LIGHTNING STRIKES.

LIGHTING SAFETY TIPS

IF YOU ARE OUTDOORS:

1. Go indoors if you can.
2. Sit in a car with the windows rolled up. Do not touch anything metal inside the car.
3. Don't stand under a tree, near water, or on high ground. Make sure you are not the tallest object around.
4. Stay away from overhead wires and metal fences.

IF YOU ARE INDOORS:

1. Stay away from open doors, windows, and fireplaces.
2. Don't use electronic devices.
3. Don't turn on faucets or touch pipes in the kitchen or bathroom.
4. Only use a telephone—landline or cellular—in emergencies.

Airplanes

On average, each large commercial airplane in operation is struck by lightning once or twice a year. But if the conditions are right, a plane may be struck several times during a single storm. In 1964, a plane circling O'Hare International Airport in Chicago, Illinois, was hit by lightning five times in 20 minutes.

An airplane's outer shell protects passengers inside from most strikes, but if a bolt hits a fuel tank or interferes with the plane's electronic navigational system, the plane may crash. Luckily, that doesn't happen very often.

Newsflash!

On December 8, 1963, a lightning bolt blasted the fuel tank of Pan American Flight 214. The plane exploded and crashed in Elkton, Maryland. All eighty-one people onboard were killed. It may have been the deadliest lightning strike in history.

The next major step in lightning research came in the 1970s. Scientists in the University of Florida's Lightning Research Group developed a lightning detection network that tracks cloud-to-ground lightning strikes throughout the continental United States—24 hours a day, 365 days a year.

Special sensors at more than one hundred stations located throughout the country record lightning strikes. Since 1989, the information has been relayed to a data collection center in Tucson, Arizona. Computers analyze the data and send out warnings, so weather forecasters can alert people living in the area of a storm. The information is also used by people who work at outdoor recreation centers and electric power stations, air traffic controllers, and park rangers who monitor forests for wildfires.

Data recorded by National Lightning Detection Network sensors, such as this one (above), is analyzed and stored at the Network Control Center in Tucson, Arizona. Then it is relayed to meteorologists all over the United States. They combine that information with satellite data to create computer-generated weather maps, like these at the National Weather Service in Boise, Idaho (left).

The Heart of the Storm

Lightning is dangerous and unpredictable. And even though scientists have spent many years studying it, they still have a lot to learn.

"We know a lot about the lightning flash once it gets going," says Dave Rust, a retired researcher at the National Severe Storm Lab in Norman, Oklahoma, "but what makes it start? We don't know how you get a big enough electrical field [for a stepped leader to form]."

To find out, scientists release weather balloons into the hearts of thunderheads. The balloons carry special equipment that can measure the electric fields inside and surrounding the clouds. Even though the summer storm season is short and wind and hail often ruin their experiments, the researchers are beginning to make some important discoveries.

In Florida, engineer Phil Barker has studied the effect of lightning strikes on aboveground

Scientists use weather balloons in many different ways. In this photo, Stephen Ezell, a meteorological systems operator at Cape Canaveral Air Force Station in Florida, is releasing a balloon that will measure the air's temperature and humidity as it rises.

Engineer George Schnetzer prepares equipment for rockets that will be launched to trigger lightning at the University of Florida's International Center for Lightning Research and Testing at the Camp Blanding National Guard near Starke, Florida. His team's results will be used to develop new ways to protect aircraft against lightning strikes.

and underground power lines for the Electrical Power Research Institute. He and his team built a miniature version of a town's entire electrical power system. The team attracted lightning to the "town" by launching a small rocket with a wire attached into a thunderhead. If the rocket triggered a lightning stroke, a trail of negative charges followed the wire to the model town's power lines.

"A lot of people thought that because underground power cables are buried . . . that there shouldn't be much of a problem," says Barker. But it turns out that lightning can follow the lines underground and destroy them. According to Barker, ". . . underground cables are affected by lightning significantly."

This amazing image shows lightning that was triggered by a rocket on June 4, 2009. The strike is stretched wide because as the negative charges race down the copper wire on the left, the wind blows them to the right. The bright jagged line (far right) consists of five return strokes that occurred during the six seconds the camera's shutter was open.

Clues to the Past

If a lightning stroke stays in contact with sandy soil long enough, it can melt the minerals in sand. When the melted material cools, it fuses to form a hollow, glass-lined tube that marks the lightning's path across the ground. These tubes, called fulgurites, can be up to 3 inches (7.5 centimeters) across and several feet long.

This illustration shows how a lightning strike forms a fulgurite in sandy soil.

Researchers carefully excavated this fulgurite in Central Florida.

In 2007, Rafael Navarro-González, a chemist at the National Autonomous University of Mexico in Mexico City, Mexico, decided to study a fulgurite from the Sahara, a desert in northern Africa. Thunderstorms are rare in the Sahara, yet many fulgurites have been found there. Navarro-González wondered why.

When he noticed tiny bubbles along the fulgurite's inner surface, he carefully opened them with a laser and discovered gases that had formed when lightning's heat vaporized bits of decaying plant material in the sandy soil. It turns out the rotting material had come from grasses and shrubs that usually grow in hot, semi-arid environments. These results suggested that when the lightning strike occurred, the landscape was less dry and less harsh than it is today.

Next, Navarro-González asked Shannon Mahan, a scientist at the U.S. Geological Survey in Denver, Colorado, to test the fulgurite to find out when it formed. Mahan came up with a surprising answer: The fulgurite was about 15,000 years old. Because fulgurites are so fragile, no one had thought they could survive that long.

"It's an exciting discovery," says Navarro-González. "I hope this work will spur scientists to take a closer look at all the fulgurites that have been sitting in museum drawers and display cases for decades."

Scientists collected these fulgurites in Nigeria, a country on the west coast of Africa.

Lightning in Space

Earth isn't the only place in space with lightning. Equipment onboard spacecraft have captured images that prove bolts of electricity rip through the skies above Jupiter, Venus, and Saturn. Data from spacecraft suggest that Neptune and Uranus probably have lightning too.

Here's your chance to take a look at some lightning activity that's out of this world. Scientists are learning more about it every day.

Jupiter

The *Voyager*, *Galileo*, and *Cassini* space probes have all sent back images that show evidence of gigantic thunderstorms with electrifying lightning strikes high in Jupiter's atmosphere. Scientists believe that lightning is less common on Jupiter than it is on Earth, but that each bolt delivers about ten times more energy. These images, which *Galileo* recorded in October 1997, show lightning flashes as white spots.

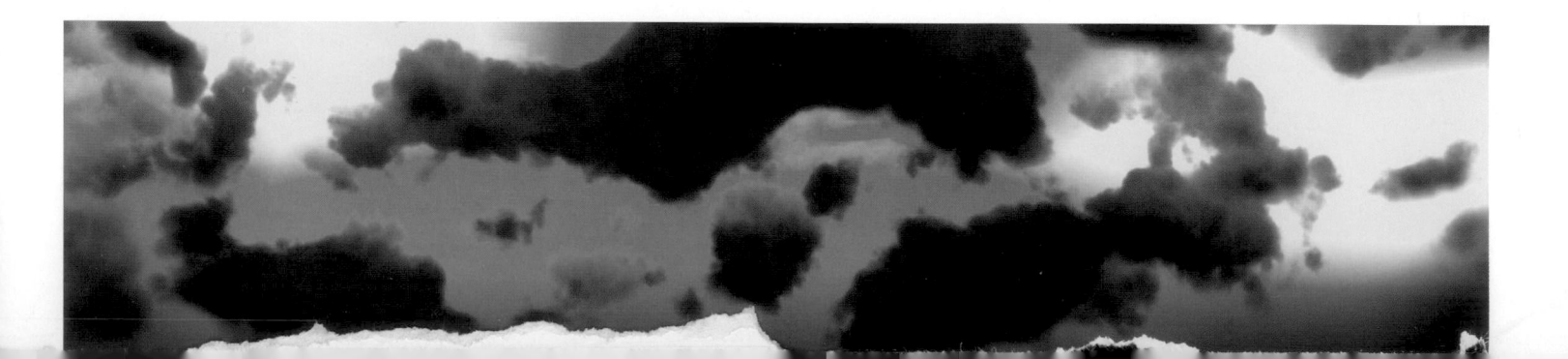

Venus

In 2007, the European Space Agency's *Venus Express* spacecraft detected lightning on Venus. Our sister planet's bolts don't come from clouds of water droplets. They are produced by the clouds of sulfuric acid that fill Venus's atmosphere. This artist's representation of what the storm might look like helps us get a sense of its power.

Saturn

After the *Cassini* spacecraft spotted a thunderstorm with lightning on Saturn, both amateur and professional astronomers on Earth began monitoring it. Trevor Barry, an amateur stargazer in Australia, estimated that the storm generated "thousands, probably hundreds of thousands [of lightning bolts] every second." Experts believe the storm was around ten thousand times more powerful than any seen on Earth. In this image, the colors of the planet are enhanced so that the storm can be seen more easily.

Words to Know

atmosphere the layer of air and other gases that surrounds a planet

ball lightning a glowing sphere of electricity that hovers in place or floats or bobs through the air

blue jets in meteorology, dim, blue streaks of light that burst out of a thunderhead, arc upward into the atmosphere, and then fade away

bolt from the blue positively charged energy released from the top of a distant thunderhead. It may travel horizontally for several miles before swerving downward to connect with a streamer.

condense to change from a gas to a liquid

dart leader a stream of electricity that travels straight down a lightning channel to the ground after a return stroke has been discharged

discharge to release, or give off, energy

elve in meteorology, a flat disk of dim light that forms about 60 miles (96 km) above Earth's surface following a very energetic lightning strike. It radiates out in every direction

fulgurite a hollow, glass-lined tube that forms when lightning stays in contact with sandy soil for approximately a full second

lightning channel a path of flowing electricity that forms when a stepped leader meets a streamer

red sprite in meteorology, red light that shoots up from a thunderhead following a very energetic lightning strike

return stroke a surge of negative electrical charges that flow from a thunderhead through a lightning channel to the ground. It creates the flash we call lightning.

sheet lightning distant lightning reflected off clouds or scattered by water droplets in the air. The flash brightens a broad area of sky.

St. Elmo's fire an eerie blue, green, or purplish glow that appears around a flagpole, the wing of an airplane, or the mast of a ship as negative electric charges in the air are pulled toward the positively charged object

stepped leader an invisible, negatively charged spark that darts out of a cloud and branches in many directions in search of positive electrical charges on the ground

streamer a positively charged electric spark that races up from the ground or a tall object to meet a stepped leader

water vapor water that has turned into a gas. Clouds are made of water vapor.

Find Out More

Websites to Visit

Bright Light Fright: Lightning
http://sln.fi.edu/weather/lightning/lightning.html

History and Mystery of Lightning
http://www.lightningsafety.noaa.gov/history.htm

Lightning Science and Safety
http://www.usatoday.com/weather/resources/basics/wlightning.htm

Lightning: The Shocking Story
http://www.nationalgeographic.com/features/96/lightning/index.html

Books to Read

Lightning, Hurricanes, and Blizzards: The Science of Storms by Paul Fleisher (Lerner Publications, 2010).

Lightning by Seymour Simon (HarperCollins, 2006).

Video to Watch

Lightning! Nature's Most Dazzling and Dangerous Display (WGBH Education Foundation, 60 min., 2004).

Bibliography

Barnes-Svarney, Patricia, and Thomas E. Svarney. *Skies of Fury: Weather Weirdness Around the World.* New York: Touchstone/Simon & Schuster, 1999.

Bowden, Rich. "Outback Astronomer Records Saturn Storm for NASA." *The Tech Herald.* May 24, 2008. http://www.thetechherald.com/article.php/200818/887/Outback-astronomer-records-Saturn-storm-for-NASA.

Burt, Christopher C. *Extreme Weather: A Guide and Record Book.* New York: W.W. Norton & Company, 2007.

Douglas, Paul. *Restless Skies: The Ultimate Weather Book.* New York: Sterling Publishing, 2005.

Fink, Micah. "How Lightning Forms." and "Current Lightning Research." *Savage Planet: Deadly Skies.* WGBH. http://www.pbs.org/wnet/savageplanet/index.html.

The Franklin Institute Resources for Learning. "Bright Light Fright: Lightning." http://sln.fi.edu/weather/lightning/lightning.html.

Gibbs, W. Wayt. "Sprites and Elves: Lightning's Strange Cousins Flicker Faster than Light Itself." *Scientific American.* http://www-star.stanford.edu/~vlf/optical/press/elves97sciam/.

"History and Mystery of Lightning." National Weather Service. http://www.lightningsafety.noaa.gov/history.htm.

Lightning! Nature's Most Dazzling and Dangerous Display. Boston: WGBH Education Foundation, 60 min., 2004.

"A Lightning Primer." Lightning & Atmospheric Electricity Research at the Global Hydrology and Climate Center, National Aeronautics and Space Administration (NASA). http://thunder.msfc.nasa.gov/primer/.

"Lightning: The Shocking Story." National Geographic Society. http://www.nationalgeographic.com/features/96/lightning/index.html.

Mogil, H. Michael. *Extreme Weather.* New York: Black Dog & Leventhal Publishers, 2007.

Navarro-González, Rafael (Professor of Chemistry, National Autonomous University of Mexico, Mexico City, Mexico) personal interview, February 25, 2007.

Witze, Alexandra. "When Dust Swirls and Lightning Zaps," *Science News,* May 8, 2010.

Source Notes

Page 25: "I saw a . . . floor and disappeared." Dorothy Stewart, Dennis Port, MA, personal interview, July 2, 2010.

Page 25: "I saw it . . . and faded away." Bruce Stewart, Dennis Port, MA, personal interview, July 2, 2010.

Page 29: "I was pushed . . . sliced in two." Barnes-Svarney, Patricia, and Thomas E. Svarney. *Skies of Fury: Weather Weirdness Around the World.* (Touchstone/Simon & Schuster, 1999).

Page 31: "[T]here was a . . . what had happened." Tal Alter, personal interview, October 1, 2010.

Page 32: "Immersed in the . . . on the ground." Michael McQuilken, personal interview, March 6, 2011.

Page 40: "We know a . . . leader to form]." *Lightning! Nature's Most Dazzling and Dangerous Display.* (WGBH Education Foundation, 2004).

Page 41: "A lot of . . . by lightning significantly." *Lightning! Nature's Most Dazzling and Dangerous Display.* (WGBH Education Foundation, 2004).

Page 44: "thousands, probably hundreds . . . [bolts] every second." Bowden, Rich. "Outback Astronomer Records Saturn Storm for NASA." *The Tech Herald.* May 24, 2008. http://www.thetechherald.com/article.php/200818/887/Outback-astronomer-records-Saturn-storm-for-NASA.

Page 45: "It's an exciting . . . cases for decades." Rafael Navarro-González (Professor of Chemistry, National Autonomous University of Mexico, Mexico City, Mexico), personal interview, February 25, 2007.

Index